MYTH AND MEANING

Myth
and Meaning

Claude Lévi-Strauss

Routledge & Kegan Paul
London and Henley

First published in Great Britain in 1978
by Routledge & Kegan Paul Ltd
39 Store Street,
London WC1E 7DD and
Broadway House,
Newtown Road,
Henley-on-Thames,
Oxon RG9 1EN
Printed in Great Britain by
Lowe & Brydone Printers Ltd
Thetford, Norfolk
© University of Toronto Press 1978

British Library Cataloguing in Publication Data

Lévi-Strauss, Claude

Myth and meaning.
1. Mythology   2. Structuralism
I. Title
291. 1'3   BL311

ISBN 0 7100 0104 5

The 1977 Massey Lectures

Ever since the advent of science in the seventeenth century, we have rejected mythology as a product of superstitious and primitive minds. Only now are we coming to a fuller appreciation of the nature and role of myth in human history. In these five lectures, the distinguished social anthropologist, Claude Lévi-Strauss, offers the insights of a lifetime spent interpreting myths and trying to discover their significance for human understanding.

Entitled 'Myth and Meaning,' the talks were broadcast on the CBC Radio series, *Ideas*, in December 1977. They were assembled from a series of lengthy conversations between Professor Lévi-Strauss and Carole Orr Jerome, producer in the Paris bureau of the CBC. The programs were organized by Geraldine Sherman, executive producer of *Ideas*, and produced by Bernie Lucht.

The lectures have been expanded for publication to include some material which, for reasons of time, could not be used in the original broadcasts. The spoken words have been minimally edited to make

them conform to the more rigid conventions of print.
Carole Orr Jerome's main questions to Professor
Lévi-Strauss, which helped shape the course of the
lectures, were as follows:

CHAPTER ONE

Many of your readers think that you are trying to
bring us back to mythical thought, that we have lost
something very precious and that we must try to gain
it back. Does this mean that science and modern
thought must go out the window and that we must
go back to mythical thought?

What is structuralism? How did you arrive at the
idea that structural thought was a possibility?

Is it necessary to have order and rules to have
meaning? Can you have meaning in chaos? What do
you mean that order is preferable to disorder?

CHAPTERS TWO AND THREE

There are those who say that the thinking of so-called
primitive people is inferior to scientific thinking. They
say that it is inferior, not because of a matter of style,
but because, scientifically speaking, it is wrong. How
would you compare 'primitive' thought with 'scientific' thought?

Aldous Huxley, in his discussion in *The Doors of
Perception*, said that most of us use only a certain
amount of our mental powers and the rest of them
are completely shut away. Do you feel that in the
kind of lives we lead today, we are using less of our

mental capacities than the people you write of who thought in a mythical fashion?

Nature shows us a variegated world, and we've tended to pick up on the differences between us rather than the similarities in the development of our cultures. Do you think we are developing to a point where we can start closing many of the divisions that exist between us?

CHAPTER FOUR

There is the old problem of the investigator who changes the subject of his investigation by simply being there. In looking at our collections of mythological stories, do they have meaning and order of their own, or has order been imposed by the anthropologists who have collected the stories?

What is the difference between the conceptual organization of mythological thinking and that of history? Does the mythological telling of a story deal with historical facts, then transform them and use them in another way?

CHAPTER FIVE

Could you talk in general about the relationship between myth and music?

You have said that both myth and music stem from language but evolve in different directions. What do you mean by this?

Contents

Contents

MYTH AND MEANING

An Introduction

Although I am going to talk about what I have written, my books and papers and so on, unfortunately I forget what I have written practically as soon as it is finished. There is probably going to be some trouble about that. But nevertheless I think there is also something significant about it, in that I don't have the feeling that I write my books. I have the feeling that my books get written through me and that once they have got across me I feel empty and nothing is left.

You may remember that I have written that myths get thought in man unbeknownst to him. This has been much discussed and even criticized by my English-speaking colleagues, because their feeling is that, from an empirical point of view, it is an utterly meaningless sentence. But for me it describes a lived experience, because it says exactly how I perceive my own relationship to my work. That is, my work gets thought in me unbeknown to me.

I never had, and still do not have, the perception of feeling my personal identity. I appear to myself as the place where something is going on, but there is no 'I', no 'me.' Each of us is a kind of crossroads where things happen. The crossroads is purely passive; something happens there. A different thing, equally valid, happens elsewhere. There is no choice, it is just a matter of chance.

I don't pretend at all that, because I think that way, I am entitled to conclude that mankind thinks that way too. But I believe that, for each scholar and each writer, the particular way he or she thinks and writes opens a new outlook on mankind. And the fact that I personally have this idiosyncracy perhaps entitles me to point to something which is valid, while the way in which my colleagues think opens different outlooks, all of which are equally valid.

ONE

The Meeting of Myth and Science

Let me start with a personal confession. There is a magazine which I read faithfully each month from the first line to the last, even though I don't understand all of it; it is the *Scientific American*. I am extremely eager to be as informed as possible of everything that takes place in modern science and its new developments. My position in relation to science is thus not a negative one.

Secondly, I think there are some things we have lost, and we should try perhaps to regain them, because I am not sure that in the kind of world in which we are living and with the kind of scientific thinking we are bound to follow, we can regain these things exactly as if they had never been lost; but we can try to become aware of their existence and their importance.

In the third place, my feeling is that modern science is not at all moving away from these lost things, but that more and more it is attempting to reintegrate them in the field of scientific explanation. The real gap, the real separation between science and what we might as well call mythical thought for the sake of finding a convenient name, although it is not exactly that – the real separation occurred in the seventeenth and the eighteenth century. At that time, with Bacon, Descartes, Newton, and the others, it was necessary for science to build itself up against the old generations of mythical and mystical thought, and it was thought that science could only exist by turning its back upon the world of the senses, the world we see, smell, taste, and perceive; the sensory was a delusive world, whereas the real world was a world of mathematical properties which could only be grasped by the intellect and which was entirely at odds with the false testimony of the senses. This was probably a necessary move, for experience shows us that thanks to this separation – this schism if you like – scientific thought was able to constitute itself.

Now, my impression (and, of course, I do not talk as a scientist – I am not a physicist, I am not a biologist, I am not a chemist) is that contemporary science is tending to overcome this gap, and that more and more the sense data are being reintegrated into scientific explanation as something which has a meaning, which has a truth, and which can be explained.

Take, for instance, the world of smells. We were accustomed to think that this was entirely subjective, outside the world of science. Now the chemists are able to tell us that each smell or each taste has a certain chemical composition and to give us the reasons why subjectively some smells or some tastes feel to us as having something in common and some others seem widely different.

Let's take another example. There was in philosophy from the time of the Greeks to the eighteenth and even the nineteenth century – and there still is to some extent – a tremendous discussion about the origin of mathematical ideas – the idea of the line, the idea of the circle, the idea of the triangle. There were, in the main, two classical theories: one of the mind as a *tabula rasa*, with nothing in it in the beginning; everything comes to it from experience. It is from seeing a lot of round objects, none of which were perfectly round, that we are able nevertheless to abstract the idea of the circle. The second classical theory goes back to Plato, who claimed that such ideas of the circle, of the triangle, of the line, are perfect, innate in the mind, and it is because they are given to the mind that we are able to project them, so to speak, on reality, although reality never offers us a perfect circle or a perfect triangle.

Now, contemporary researchers on the neurophysiology of vision teach us that the nervous cells in the retina and the other apparatus behind the retina are specialized: some cells are sensitive only to straight direction, in the vertical sense, others in the horizontal, others in the oblique, some of them to the relationship between the background and the central figures, and the like. So – and I simplify very much because it is too complicated for me to explain this in

English – this whole problem of experience versus mind seems to have a solution in the structure of the nervous system, not in the structure of the mind or in experience, but somewhere between mind and experience in the way our nervous system is built and in the way it mediates between mind and experience.

Probably there is something deep in my own mind, which makes it likely that I always was what is now being called a structuralist. My mother told me that, when I was about two years old and still unable to read, of course, I claimed that actually I was able to read. And when I was asked why, I said that when I looked at the signboards on shops – for instance, *boulanger* (baker) or *boucher* (butcher) – I was able to read something because what was obviously similar, from a graphic point of view, in the writing could not mean anything other than 'bou,' the same first syllable of *boucher* and *boulanger*. Probably there is nothing more than that in the structuralist approach; it is the quest for the invariant, or for the invariant elements among superficial differences.

Throughout my life, this search was probably a predominant interest of mine. When I was a child, for a while my main interest was geology. The problem in geology is also to try to understand what is invariant in the tremendous diversity of landscapes, that is, to be able to reduce a landscape to a finite number of geological layers and of geological operations. Later as an adolescent, I spent a great part of my leisure time drawing costumes and sets for opera. The problem there is exactly the same - to try to express in one language, that is, the language of graphic arts and painting, something which also exists in music and in the libretto; that is, to try to reach the invariant property of a very complex set of codes (the musical code, the literary code, the artistic code). The problem is to find what is common to all of them. It's a problem, one might say, of translation, of translating what is expressed in one language - or one code, if you prefer, but language is sufficient - into expression in a different language.

Structuralism, or whatever goes under that name, has been considered as something completely new and at the time revolutionary; this, I think, is doubly false. In the first place, even in the field of the humanities, it is not new at all; we can follow very well this trend of thought from the Renaissance to the nineteenth century and to the present time. But it is also wrong for another reason: what we call structuralism in the field of linguistics, or anthropology, or the like, is nothing other than a very pale and faint imitation of what the 'hard sciences,' as I think you call them in English, have been doing all the time.

Science has only two ways of proceeding: it is either reductionist or structuralist. It is reductionist when it is possible to find out that very complex phenomena on one level can be reduced to simpler phenomena on other levels. For instance, there is a lot in life which can be reduced to physicochemical processes, which explain a part but not all. And when we are

confronted with phenomena too complex to be reduced to phenomena of a lower order, then we can
only approach them by looking to their relationships,
that is, by trying to understand what kind of original
system they make up. This is exactly what we have
been trying to do in linguistics, in anthropology, and
in different fields.

It is true - and let's personalize nature for the sake
of the argument - that Nature has only a limited number of procedures at her disposal and that the kinds of
procedure which Nature uses at one level of reality are
bound to reappear at different levels. The genetic
code is a very good example; it is well known that,
when the biologists and the geneticists had the problem of describing what they had discovered, they
could do nothing better than borrow the language of
linguistics and to speak of words, of phrase, of accent,
of punctuation marks, and the like. I do not mean at
all that it is the same thing; of course, it is not. But it
is the same kind of problem arising at two different
levels of reality.

It would be very far from my mind to try to reduce
culture, as we say in our anthropological jargon, to nature; but nevertheless what we witness at the level of
culture are phenomena of the same kind from a *for-
mal* point of view (I do not mean at all substantially).
We can at least trace the same problem to the mind
that we can observe on the level of nature, though, of
course, the cultural is much more complicated and
calls upon a much larger number of variables.

I'm not trying to formulate a philosophy, or even a theory. Since I was a child, I have been bothered by, let's call it the irrational, and have been trying to find an order behind what is given to us as a disorder. It so happened that I became an anthropologist, as a matter of fact not because I was interested in anthropology, but because I was trying to get out of philosophy. It also so happened that in the French academic framework, where anthropology was at the time not taught as a discipline in its own right in the universities, it was possible for somebody trained in philosophy and teaching philosophy to escape to anthropology. I escaped there, and was confronted immediately by one problem – there were lots of rules of marriage all over the world which looked absolutely meaningless, and it was all the more irritating because, if they were meaningless, then there should be different rules for each people, though nevertheless the number of rules could be more or less finite. So, if the same absurdity was found to reappear over and over again, and another kind of absurdity also to reappear, then this was something which was not absolutely absurd; otherwise it would not reappear.

Such was my first orientation, to try to find an order behind this apparent disorder. And when after working on the kinship systems and marriage rules, I turned my attention, also by chance and not at all on purpose, toward mythology, the problem was exactly the same. Mythical stories are, or seem, arbitrary, meaningless, absurd, yet nevertheless they seem to reappear all over the world. A 'fanciful' creation of the mind in one place would be unique – you would not find the same creation in a completely different place. My problem was trying to find out if there was some kind of order behind this apparent disorder – that's all. And I do not claim that there are conclusions to be drawn.

It is, I think, absolutely impossible to conceive of meaning without order. There is something very curious in semantics, that the word 'meaning' is probably, in the whole language, the word the meaning of which is the most difficult to find. What does 'to mean' mean? It seems to me that the only answer we can give is that 'to mean' means the ability of any kind of data to be translated in a different language. I do not mean a different language like French or German, but different words on a different level. After all, this translation is what a dictionary is expected to give you – the meaning of the word in different words, which on a slightly different level are isomorphic to the word or expression you are trying to understand. Now, what would a translation be without rules? It would be absolutely impossible to understand. Because you cannot replace any word by any other word or any sentence by any other sentence, you have to have rules of translation. To speak of rules and to speak of meaning is to speak of the same thing; and if we look at all the intellectual undertakings of mankind, as far as they have been recorded all over the world, the common denominator is always to introduce some kind of order. If this represents a basic need for order in the human mind and since, after all, the human mind is only part of the universe, the need probably exists because there is some order in the universe and the universe is not a chaos.

What I have been trying to say here is that there has been a divorce - a necessary divorce - between scientific thought and what I have called the logic of the concrete, that is, the respect for and the use of the data of the senses, as opposed to images and symbols and the like. We are witnessing the moment when this divorce will perhaps be overcome or reversed, because modern science seems to be able to make progress not only in its own traditional line - pushing forward and forward but still within the same narrow channel - but also at the same time to widen the channel and to reincorporate a great many problems previously left outside.

In this respect, I may be subjected to the criticism of being called 'scientistic' or a kind of blind believer in science who holds that science is able to solve absolutely all problems. Well, I certainly don't believe that, because I cannot conceive that a day will come when science will be complete and achieved. There will always be new problems, and exactly at the same pace as science is able to solve problems which were deemed philosophical a dozen years or a century ago, so there will appear new problems which had not hitherto been not perceived as such. There will always be a gap between the answer science is able to give us and the new question which this answer will raise. So I am not 'scientistic' in that way. Science will never give us all the answers. What we can try to do is to increase very slowly the number and the quality of the answers we are able to give, and this, I think, we can do only through science.

TWO

'Primitive' Thinking and the 'Civilized' Mind

The way of thinking among people we call, usually and wrongly, 'primitive' - let's describe them rather as 'without writing,' because I think this is really the discriminatory factor between them and us - has been interpreted in two different fashions, both of which in my opinion were equally wrong. The first way was to consider such thinking as of a somewhat coarser quality, and in contemporary anthropology the example which comes to mind immediately is the work of Malinowski. I must say immediately that I have the greatest respect for him and consider him a very great anthropologist, and I'm not at all deriding his contribution. But nevertheless the feeling in Malinowski was that the thought of the people he was studying was, and generally speaking the thought of all the populations without writing which are the subject matter of anthropology was entirely, or is, determined by the basic needs of life. If you know that a people, whoever they are, is determined by the bare necessities of living - finding subsistence, satisfying the sexual drives, and so on – then you can explain their social institutions, their beliefs, their mythology, and the like. This very widespread conception in anthropology generally goes under the name of functionalism.

The other fashion is not so much that theirs is an inferior kind of thought, but a fundamentally different kind of thought. This approach is exemplified by the work of Lévy-Bruhl, who considered that the basic difference between 'primitive' thought – I always put the word 'primitive' within quotes – and modern thought is that the first is entirely determined by emotion and mystic representations. Whereas Malinowski's is a utilitarian conception, the other is an emotional or affective conception; and what I have tried to emphasize is that actually the thought of people without writing is, or can be in many instances, on the one hand, disinterested – and this is a difference in relation to Malinowski – and, on the other hand, intellectual – a difference in relation to Lévy-Bruhl.

What I tried to show in *Totemism* and in *The Savage Mind*, for instance, is that these people whom we usually consider as completely subservient to the need of not starving, of continuing able just to subsist in very harsh material conditions, are perfectly capable of disinterested thinking; that is, they are moved by a need or a desire to understand the world around them, its nature and their society. On the other hand, to achieve that end, they proceed by intellectual means, exactly as a philosopher, or even to some extent a scientist, can and would do.

This is my basic hypothesis.

I would like to dispel a misunderstanding right away. To say that a way of thinking is disinterested and that it is an intellectual way of thinking does not mean at all that it is equal to scientific thinking. Of course, it remains different in a way, and inferior in another way. It remains different because its aim is to reach by the shortest possible means a general understanding of the universe – and not only a general but a *total* understanding. That is, it is a way of thinking which must imply that if you don't understand everything, you don't explain anything. This is entirely in contradiction to what scientific thinking does, which is to proceed step by step, trying to give explanations for very limited phenomena, and then going on to other kinds of phenomena, and so on. As Descartes had already said, scientific thinking aimed to divide the difficulty into as many parts as were necessary in order to solve it.

So this totalitarian ambition of the savage mind is quite different from the procedures of scientific thinking. Of course, the great difference is that this ambition does not succeed. We are able, through scientific thinking, to achieve mastery over nature – I don't need to elaborate that point, it is obvious enough – while, of course, myth is unsuccessful in giving man more material power over the environment. However, it gives man, very importantly, the illusion that he can understand the universe and that he *does* understand the universe. It is, of course, only an illusion.

We should note, however, that as scientific thinkers we use a very limited amount of our mental power. We use what is needed by our profession, our trade, or the particular situation in which we are involved at the moment. So, if somebody gets involved for twenty years and even more in the way myths or kinship systems operate, then he uses this part of his mental power. But we cannot request that each of us be interested in exactly the same things; so each of us uses a certain amount of our mental power for what is needed or for what interests us.

Today we use less and we use more of our mental capacity than we did in the past; And it is not exactly the same kind of mental capacity as it was either. For example, we use considerably less of our sensory perceptions. When I was writing the first version of *Mythologiques* (*Introduction to a Science of Mythology*), I was confronted with a problem which to me was extremely mysterious. It seems that there was a particular tribe which was able to see the planet Venus in full daylight, something which to me would be utterly impossible and incredible. I put the question to professional astronomers; they told me, of course, that we don't but, nevertheless, when we know the amount of light emitted by the planet Venus in full daylight, it was not absolutely inconceivable that some people could. Later on I looked into old treatises on navigation belonging to our own civilization and it seems that sailors of old were perfectly able to see the planet in full daylight. Probably we could still do so if we had a trained eye.

It is exactly the same with our knowledge about plants or animals. People who are without writing have a fantastically precise knowledge of their environment and all their resources. All these things we have lost, but we did not lose them for nothing; we are now able to drive an automobile without being crushed at each moment, for example, or in the evening to turn on our television or radio. This implies a training of mental capacities which 'primitive' peoples don't have because they don't need them. I feel that, with the potential they have, they could have changed the quality of their mind, but it would not be needed for the kind of life and relationship to nature that they have. You cannot develop all the mental capacities belonging to mankind all at once. You can only use a small sector, and this sector is not the same according to the culture. That is all.

It is probably one of the many conclusions of anthropological research that, notwithstanding the cultural differences between the several parts of mankind, the human mind is everywhere one and the same and that it has the same capacities. I think this is accepted everywhere.

I don't think that cultures have tried systematically or methodically to differentiate themselves from each other. The fact is that for hundreds of thousands of years mankind was not very numerous on the earth; small groups were living in isolation, so that it was only natural that they developed characteristics of their own and became different from each other. It was not something aimed at. Rather, it is the simple result of the conditions which have been prevailing for an extremely long time.

Now, I would not like you to think that this in itself is harmful or that these differences should be overcome. As a matter of fact, differences are extremely fecund. It is only through difference that progress has been made. What threatens us right now is probably what we may call over-communication – that is, the tendency to know exactly in one point of the world what is going on in all other parts of the world. In order for a culture to be really itself and to produce something, the culture and its members must be convinced of their originality and even, to some extent, of their superiority over the others; it is only under conditions of under-communication that it can produce anything. We are now threatened with the prospect of our being only consumers, able to consume anything from any point in the world and from every culture, but of losing all originality.

We can easily now conceive of a time when there will be only one culture and one civilization on the entire surface of the earth. I don't believe this will happen, because there are contradictory tendencies always at work – on the one hand towards homogenization and on the other towards new distinctions. The more a civilization becomes homogenized, the more internal lines of separation become apparent; and what is gained on one level is immediately lost on another. This is a personal feeling, in that I have no clear proof of the operation of this dialectic. But I don't see how mankind can really live without some internal diversity.

Let us now consider a myth from western Canada about the skate trying to master or dominate the South Wind and succeeding. It is a story of a time that existed on earth before mankind, that is, of a time when animals and humans were not really distinct; beings were half-human and half-animal. All were extremely bothered by the winds, because the winds, especially the bad winds, were blowing all the time, making it impossible for them to fish and to gather shellfish on the beaches. So they decided that they had to fight the winds and compel them to behave more decently. There was an expedition in which several human animals or animal humans took part, including the skate, which played an important role in capturing the South Wind. The South Wind was liberated only after he promised not to blow all the time, but only from time to time, or at certain periods. Since that time, it is only at certain periods of the year, or one day out of two, that the South Wind blows; during the rest of the time, mankind can fulfil its activities.

Well, this story never happened. But what we have to do is not to satisfy ourselves that this is plainly absurd or just a fanciful creation of a mind in a kind of delirium. We have to take it seriously and to ask ourselves the questions: why the skate and why the South Wind?

When you look very closely at the mythical material

exactly as it is told, you notice that the skate acts on account of very precise characteristics, which are of two kinds. The first one is that it is a fish like all flat fish, slippery underneath and rough on the back. And the other capacity, which allow the skate to escape very successfully when it has to fight against other animals, is that it is very large seen from above or below, and extremely thin when seen from the side. An adversary may think that it is very easy to shoot an arrow and kill a skate because it is so large; but just as the arrow is being aimed, the skate can suddenly turn or slip and show only its profile, which, of course, is impossible to aim at; thus it escapes. So the reason why the skate is chosen is that it is an animal which, considered from either one point of view or from the other, is capable of giving - let's say in terms of cybernetics - only a 'yes' or 'no' answer. It is capable of two states which are discontinuous, and one is positive, and one is negative. The use the skate is put to in the myth is - though, of course, I would not like to strain the simile too far - like the elements in modern computers which can be used to solve very difficult problems by adding a series of 'yes' or 'no' answers.

While it is obviously wrong and impossible from an empirical point of view that a fish is able to fight a wind, from a logical point of view we can understand why *images* borrowed from experience can be put to use. This is the originality of mythical thinking - to play the part of conceptual thinking: an animal which can be used as what I would call a binary operator can have, from a logical point of view, a relationship with a problem which is also a binary problem. If the South Wind blows every day of the year, then life is impossible for mankind. But if it blows only one day out of two – 'yes' one day, 'no' the other day, and so on – then a kind of compromise becomes possible between the needs of mankind and the conditions prevailing in the natural world.

Thus, from a logical point of view, there is an affinity between an animal like the skate and the kind of problem which the myth is trying to solve. The story is not true from a scientific point of view, but we could only understand this property of the myth at a time when cybernetics and computers have come to exist in the scientific world and have provided us with an understanding of binary operations which had already been put to use in a very different way with concrete objects or beings by mythical thought. So there is really not a kind of divorce between mythology and science. It is only the present state of scientific thought that gives us the ability to understand what is in this myth, to which we remained completely blind before the idea of binary operations become familiar to us.

Now, I would not like you to think that I am putting scientific explanation and mythical explanation on an equal footing. What I would say is that the greatness and the superiority of scientific explanation lies not only in the practical and intellectual achievement of science, but in the fact, which we are witnessing more and more, that science is becoming able to explain not only its own validity but also what was to some extent valid in mythological thinking. What is important is that we are becoming more and more interested in this qualitative aspect, and that science, which had a purely quantitative outlook in the seventeenth to nineteenth centuries, is beginning to integrate the qualitative aspects of reality as well. This undoubtedly will enable us to understand a great many things present in mythological thinking which we were in the past prone to dismiss as meaningless and absurd. And the trend will lead us to believe that, between life and thought, there is not the absolute gap which was accepted as a matter of fact by the seventeenth-century philosophical dualism. If we are led to believe that what takes place in our mind is something not substantially or fundamentally different from the basic phenomenon of life itself, and if we are led then to the feeling that there is not this kind of gap which is impossible to overcome between mankind on the one hand and all the other living beings - not only animals, but also plants - on the other, then perhaps we will reach more wisdom, let us say, than we think we are capable of.

THREE

Harelips and Twins: The Splitting of a Myth

Our starting point here will be a puzzling observation recorded by a Spanish missionary in Peru, Father P.J. de Arriaga, at the end of the sixteenth century, and published in his *Extirpacion de la Idolatria del Peru* (Lima 1621). He noted that in a certain part of Peru of his time, in times of bitter cold the priest called in all the inhabitants who were known to have been born feet first, or who had a harelip, or who were twins. They were accused of being responsible for the cold because, it was said, they had eaten salt and peppers, and they were ordered to repent and to confess their sins.

Now, that twins are correlated with atmospheric disorder is something very commonly accepted throughout the world, including Canada. It is well known that on the coast of British Columbia, among the Indians, twins were endowed with special powers to bring good weather, to dispel storms, and the like. This is not, however, the part of the problem which I wish to consider here. What strikes me is that all the mythographers – for instance, Sir James Frazer who quotes Arriaga in several instances – never asked the question why people with harelips and twins are considered to be similar in some respect. It seems to me that the crux of the problem is to find out: why harelips? why twins? and why are harelips and twins put together?

In order to solve the problem, we have, as sometimes happens, to make a jump from South America to North America, because it will be a North American myth which will give us the clue to the South American one. Many people have reproached me for this kind of procedure, claiming that myths of a given population can only be interpreted and understood in the framework of the culture of that given population. There are several things which I can say by way of an answer to that objection.

In the first place, it seems to me pretty obvious that, as was ascertained during recent years by the so-called Berkeley school, the population of the Americas before Columbus was much larger than it had been supposed to be. And since it was much larger, it is obvious that these large populations were to some extent in contact with one another, and that beliefs, practices, and customs were, if I may say so, seeping through. Any neighbouring population was always, to some extent, aware of what was going on in the other population. The second point in the case that we are considering here is that these myths do not exist isolated in Peru on the one hand and in Canada on the other, but that in between we find them over and over again. Really, they are pan-American myths, rather than scattered myths in different parts of the continent.

Now, among the Tupinambas, the ancient coastal Indians of Brazil at the time of the discovery, as also among the Indians of Peru, there was a myth concerning a woman, whom a very poor individual succeeded in seducing in a devious way. The best known version, recorded by the French monk André Thevet in the sixteenth century, explained that the seduced woman gave birth to twins, one of them born from the legitimate husband, and the other from the seducer, who is the Trickster. The woman was going to meet the god who would be her husband, and while on her way the Trickster intervenes and makes her believe that *he* is the god; so, she conceives from the Trickster. When she later finds the legitimate husband-to-be, she conceives from him also and later gives birth to twins. And since these false twins had different fathers, they have antithetical features: one is brave, the other a coward; one is the protector of the Indians, the other of the white people; one gives goods to the Indians, while the other one, on the contrary, is responsible for a lot of unfortunate happenings.

It so happens that in North America, we find exactly the same myth, especially in the northwest of the United States and Canada. However, in comparison with South American versions, those coming from the Canadian area show two important differences. For instance,

among the Kootenay, who live in the Rocky Moun-
tains, there is only one fecundation which has as a
consequence the birth of twins, who later on become,
one the sun, and the other the moon. And, among
some other Indians of British Columbia of the Salish
linguistic stock – the Thompson Indians and the Okan-
agan – there are two sisters who are tricked by apparently two distinct individuals, and they give birth,
each one to a son; they are not really twins because
they were born from different mothers. But since
they were born in exactly the same kind of circumstances, at least from a moral and a psychological
point of view, they are to that extent similar to twins.

Those versions are, from the point of view of what
I am trying to show, the more important. The Salish
version weakens the twin character of the hero because the twins are not brothers – they are cousins;
and it is only the circumstances of their births which
are closely parallel – they are both born thanks to a
trick. Nevertheless, the basic intention remains the
same because nowhere are the two heroes really twins;
they are born from distinct fathers, even in the South
American version, and they have opposed characters,
features which will be shown in their conduct and in
the behaviour of their descendants.

So we may say that in all cases children who are
said to be twins or believed to be twins, as in the
Kootenay verison, will have different adventures later
on which will, if I may say so, untwin them. And this
division between two individuals who are at the begin-

ning presented as twins, either real twins or equivalents to twins, is a basic characteristic of all the myths in South America or North America.

In the Salish versions of the myth, there is a very curious detail, and it is very important. You remember that in this version we have no twins whatsoever, because there are two sisters who are travelling in order to find, each one, a husband. They were told by a grandmother that they would recognize their husbands by such and such characteristics, and they are then each deluded by the Tricksters they meet on their way into believing that they are the husband whom each is supposed to marry. They spend the night with him, and each of the women will later give birth to a son.

Now, after this unfortunate night spent in the hut of the Trickster, the elder sister leaves her younger sister and goes visiting her grandmother, who is a mountain goat and also a kind of magician; for she knows in advance that her granddaughter is coming, and she sends the hare to welcome her on the road. The hare hides under a log which has fallen in the middle of the road, and when the girl lifts her leg to cross the log, the hare can have a look at her genital parts and make a very inappropriate joke. The girl is furious, and strikes him with her cane and splits his nose. This is why the animals of the leporine family now have a split nose and upper lip, which we call a harelip in people precisely on account of this anatomical peculiarity in rabbits and hares.

In other words, the elder sister starts to split the

body of the animal; if this split were carried out to the end – if it did not stop at the nose but continued through the body and to the tail – she would turn an individual into twins, that is, two individuals which are exactly similar or identical because they are both a part of a whole. In this respect, it is very important to find out what conception the American Indians all over America entertained about the origin of twins. And what we find is a general belief that twins result from an internal splitting of the body fluids which will later solidify and become the child. For instance, among some North American Indians, the pregnant woman is forbidden to turn around too fast when she is lying asleep, because if she did, the body fluids would divide in two parts, and she would give birth to twins.

There is also a myth from the Kwakiutl Indians of Vancouver Island which should be mentioned here. It tells of a small girl whom everybody hates because she has a harelip. An ogress, a supernatural cannibal woman, appears and steals all the children including the small girl with the harelip. She puts them all in her basket in order to take them home to eat them. The small girl who was taken first is at the bottom of the basket and she succeeds in splitting it open with a seashell she had picked up on the beach. The basket is on the back of the ogress, and the girl is able to drop out and run away first. She drops out *feet first.*

This position of the harelipped girl is quite symmetrical to the position of the hare in the myth which I previously mentioned: crouching beneath the heroine when he hides under the log across her path, he is in respect to her exactly in the same position as if he had been born from her and delivered feet first. So we see that there is in all this mythology an actual relationship between twins on the one hand and delivery feet first or positions which are, metaphorically speaking, identical to it on the other. This obviously clears up the connection from which we started in Father Arriaga's Peruvian relations between twins, people born feet first, and people with harelips.

The fact that the harelip is conceived as an incipient twinhood can help us to solve a problem which is quite fundamental for anthropologists working especially in Canada: why have the Ojibwa Indians and other groups of the Algonkian-speaking family selected the hare as the highest deity in which they believed? Several explanations have been brought forward: the hare was an important if not essential part of their diet; the hare runs very fast, and so was an example of the talents which the Indians should have; and so on. Nothing of that is very convincing. But if my previous interpretations were right, it seems much more convincing to say: 1, among the rodent family the hare is the larger, the more conspicuous, the more important, so it can be taken as a representative of the rodent family; 2, all rodents exhibit an anatomical peculiarity which makes out of them incipient twins, because they are partly split up.

When there are twins, or even more children, in the

womb of the mother, there is usually in the myth a very serious consequence because, even if there are only two, the children start to fight and compete in order to find out who will have the honour of being born first. And, one of them, the bad one, does not hesitate to find a short cut, if I may say so, in order to be born earlier; instead of following the natural road, he splits up the body of the mother to escape from it.

This, I think, is an explanation of why the fact of being born feet first is assimilated to twinhood, because it is in the case of twinhood that the competitive hurry of one child will make him destroy the mother in order to be the first one born. Both twinhood and delivery feet first are forerunners of a dangerous delivery, or I could even call it a heroic delivery, for the child will take the initiative and become a kind of hero, a murderous hero in some cases; but he completes a very important feat. This explains why, in several tribes, twins were killed as well as children born feet first.

The really important point is that in all American mythology, and I could say in mythology the world over, we have deities or supernaturals, who play the roles of intermediaries between the powers above and humanity below. They can be represented in different ways: we have, for instance, characters of the type of a Messiah; we have heavenly twins. And we can see that the place of the hare in Algonkian mythology is exactly between the Messiah - that is, the unique intermediary - and the heavenly twins. He is not twins, but he is incipient twins. He is still a complete individual, but he has a harelip, he is half way to becoming a twin.

This explains why, in this mythology, the hare as a god has an ambiguous character which has worried commentators and anthropologists: sometimes he is a very wise deity who is in charge of putting the universe in order, and sometimes he is a ridiculous clown who goes from mishap to mishap. And this also is best understood if we explain the choice of the hare by the Algonkian Indians as an individual who is between the two conditions of (a) a single deity beneficient to mankind and (b) twins, one of whom is good and the other bad. Being not yet entirely divided in two, being not yet twins, the two opposite characteristics can remain merged in one and the same person.

FOUR

When Myth Becomes History

This topic presents two problems for the mythologist. One is a theoretical problem of great importance because, when we look at the published material both in North and South America and elsewhere in the world, it appears that the mythic material is of two different kinds. Sometimes, anthropologists have collected myths which look more or less like shreds and patches, if I may say so; disconnected stories are put one after the other without any clear relationship between them. In other instances, as in the Vaupés area of Colombia we have very coherent mythological stories, all divided into chapters following each other in a quite logical order.

And then we have the question: what does a collection mean? It could mean two different things. It could mean, for instance, that the coherent order, like a kind of saga, is the primitive condition, and that whenever we find myths as disconnected elements, this is the result of a process of deterioration and disorganization; we can only find scattered elements of what was, earlier, a meaningful whole. Or we could hypothesize that the disconnected state was the archaic one, and that the myths were put together in an order by native wise men and philosophers who do not exist everywhere, but only in some societies of a given type. We have exactly the same problem, for instance, with the Bible, because it seems that its raw material was disconnected elements and that learned philosophers put them together in order to make a continuous story. It would be extremely important to find out if, among the people without writing who are studied by the anthropologists, the situation is the same as with the Bible or is completely different.

This second problem is, though still theoretical, of a more practical nature. In former times, let's say in the late nineteenth century and early twentieth century, mythological material was collected mostly by anthropologists, that is, people from the outside. Of course, in many cases, and especially in Canada, they had native collaborators. Let me, for instance, quote the case of Franz Boas, who had a Kwakiutl assistant, George Hunt (as a matter of fact, he was not exactly Kwakiutl because he was born of a Scottish father and a Tlingit mother, but he was raised among the Kwakiutl, married among the Kwakiutl, and completely identified with the culture). And for the Tsimshian, Boas had Henry Tate, who was a literate Tsimshian, and Marius Barbeau had William Benyon, who was also a literate Tsimshian. So native co-operation was secured from the beginning, but nevertheless the fact is that Hunt, Tate, or Benyon worked under the guidance of the anthropologists, that is, they were turned into anthropologists themselves. Of course, they knew the best legends, the traditions belonging to their own clan, their own lineage, but nevertheless they were equally interested in collecting data from other families, other clans, and the like.

When we look at this enormous corpus of Indian mythology, such as, for instance, Boas' and Tate's *Tsimshian Mythology*, or the Kwakiutl texts collected by Hunt, and edited, published, and translated too by Boas, we find more or less the same organization of the data, because it is the one which was recommended by the anthropologists: for instance, in the beginning, cosmological and cosmogonic myths, and later on, much later on, what can be considered as legendary tradition and family histories.

It has so happened that this task, started by the anthropologists, the Indians are taking now up themselves, and for different purposes, for instance, to have their language and mythology taught in elementary schools for Indian children. That is very important, I understand, at the moment. Another purpose is to use legendary tradition to validate claims against the white people - territorial claims, political claims, and so on.

So it is extremely important to find out if there is a difference and, if there is, what kind of difference between traditions collected from the outside from those collected on the inside, though *as if* they were collected from the outside. Canada is fortunate, I should say, in that books about its own mythology and legendary traditions have been organized and published by the Indian specialists themselves. This began early: there is *Legends of Vancouver* by Pauline Johnson, issued before the First World War. Later on, we had books by Marius Barbeau, who was, of course, not Indian at all, but who tried to collect historical or semihistorical material and make himself the spokesman of his Indian informants; he produced, so to speak, his own version of that mythology.

More interesting, far more interesting, are books such as *Men of Medeek*, published in Kitimat in 1962, which is supposedly the verbatim account collected from the mouth of Chief Walter Wright, a Tsimshian chief of the middle Skeena river, but collected by somebody else, a white field worker who was not even a professional. And even more important is the recent book by Chief Kenneth Harris, who is also a Tsimshian chief, published in 1974 by himself.

So we can, with this kind of material, make a kind of experiment by comparing the material collected by anthropologists, and the material collected and published directly by the Indians. I should not say 'collected,' as a matter of fact, because instead of being traditions from several families, several clans, several lineages put together and juxtaposed to each other, what we have in these two books is really the history of one family or one clan, published by one of its descendants.

The problem is: where does mythology end and where does history start? In the case, entirely new to us, of a history without archives, there being of course no written documents, there is only a verbal tradition, which is claimed to be history at the same time. Now, if we compare these two histories, the one obtained on the middle Skeena from Chief Wright, and the one written and published by Chief Harris from a family up Skeena in the Hazelton area, we find similarities and we find differences. In the account of Chief Wright, we have what I would call the genesis of a disorder: the entire story aims at explaining why after their first beginning, a given clan or lineage or group of lineages have overcome a great many ordeals, known periods of success and periods of failures, and have been progressively led towards a disastrous ending. It is an extremely pessimistic story, really the history of a downfall. In the case of Chief Harris, there is a quite different outlook, because the book appears principally geared at explaining the origin of a social order which was the social order in the historical period, and which is still embedded, if I may say so, in the several names, titles, and privileges which a given individual, occupying a prominent place in his family and clan, has collected by inheritance around himself. So it is as if a diachronic succession of events was simultaneously projected on the screen of the present in order to reconstitute piece by piece a synchronic order which exists and which is illustrated by the roster of names and privileges of a given individual.

Both stories, both books are positively fascinating, and are, literarily speaking, great pieces; but for the anthropologist, their main interest is to illustrate the characteristics of a kind of history widely different from our own. History as we write it is practically entirely based upon written documents, while in the case of these two histories there are obviously no written documents or very few. Now, what strikes me when I try to compare them is that both start with the account of a mythical or perhaps historical – I don't know which, perhaps archaeology will settle the matter – time when on the upper Skeena, near what is now Hazelton, there was a big town the name of which Barbeau transcribed as Tenlaham and an account of what happened there. It is practically the same story in both books: it explains that the city was destroyed, that the remnants of the people went on the move, and started difficult peregrinations along the Skeena.

This, of course, could be a historical event, but if we look closely at the way it is explained, we see that the type of event is the same, but not exactly the details. For instance, according to the version, there can be at the origin a fight between two villages or two towns, a fight which originated in an adultery; but the story can be either that a husband killed the lover of his wife, or that brothers killed their sister's lover, or that a husband killed his wife because she had a lover. So, you see, we have an explanatory cell. Its basic *structure* is the same, but the *content* of the cell is not the same and can vary; so it is a kind of mini-myth if

I may say so, because it is very short and very condensed, but it has still the property of a myth in that we can observe it under different transformations. When one element is transformed, then the other elements should be rearranged accordingly. This is the first aspect of these clan stories that interests me.

The second aspect is that they are histories which are highly repetitive; the same type of event can be used several times, in order to account for different happenings. For instance, it is striking that in the stories of the particular tradition of Chief Wright and of the particular tradition of Chief Harris, we find similar happenings, but they don't take place in the same spot, they don't affect the same people, and, very likely, they are not exactly in the same historical period.

What we discover by reading these books is that the opposition - the simple opposition between mythology and history which we are accustomed to make - is not at all a clear-cut one, and that there is an intermediary level. Mythology is static, we find the same mythical elements combined over and over again, but they are in a closed system, let us say, in contradistinction with history, which is, of course, an open system.

The open character of history is secured by the innumerable ways according to which mythical cells, or explanatory cells which were originally mythical, can be arranged and rearranged. It shows us that by using the same material, because it is a kind of common inheritance or common patrimony of all groups, of all clans, or of all lineages, one can nevertheless succeed in building up an original account for each of them.

What is misleading in the old anthropological accounts is that a kind of hodge-podge was made up of tradition and beliefs belonging to a great many different social groups. This makes us lose sight of a fundamental character of the material – that each type of story belongs to a given group, a given family, a given lineage, or to a given clan, and is trying to explain its fate, which can be a successful one or a disastrous one, or be intended to account for rights and privileges as they exist in the present, or be attempting to validate claims for rights which have since disappeared.

When we try to do scientific history, do we really do something scientific, or do we too remain astride our own mythology in what we are trying to make as pure history? It is very interesting to look at the way both in North and South America, and indeed everywhere in the world, in which an individual, who has by right and by inheritance a certain account of the mythology or the legendary tradition of his own group, reacts when he listens to a different version given by somebody belonging to a different family or to a different clan or lineage, which to some extent is similar but to some extent too is extremely different. Now, we would think that it is impossible that two accounts which are not the same can be true at the same time, but nevertheless, they seem to be accepted as true in some cases, the only difference made is that one account is considered better or more accurate than the other. In other cases, the two accounts can be considered equally valid because the differences between them are not perceived as such.

We are not at all aware in our daily life that we are exactly in the same situation in relation to different historical accounts written by different historians. We pay attention only to what is basically similar, and we neglect the differences due to the fact that the way historians carve the data and the way they interpret them are not exactly the same. So if you take two accounts by historians, with different intellectual traditions and different political leanings, of such events as the American Revolution, of the French-English war in Canada, or the French Revolution, we are not really so shocked that they don't tell us exactly the same thing.

Thus my impression is that by studying carefully this history, in the general sense of the word, which contemporary Indian authors try to give us of their own past, by not considering this history as a fanciful account, but by trying extremely carefully, with the help of a type of salvage archaeology - excavating village sites referred to in the histories - and by trying to establish correspondences, inasmuch as this is possible, between different accounts, and by trying to find what really corresponds and what does not correspond, we may in the end reach a better understanding of what historical science really is.

I am not far from believing that, in our own societies,

history has replaced mythology and fulfils the same function, that for societies without writing and without archives the aim of mythology is to ensure that as closely as possible – complete closeness is obviously impossible – the future will remain faithful to the present and to the past. For us, however, the future should be always different, and ever more different, from the present, some difference depending, of course, on our political preferences. But nevertheless the gap which exists in our mind to some extent between mythology and history can probably be breached by studying histories which are conceived as not at all separated from but as a continuation of mythology.

FIVE

Myth and Music

The relationship between myth and music on which I insisted so much in the initial section of *The Raw and the Cooked* and also in the final section of *L'Homme nu* - there is not yet an English title because it is not translated - was probably the topic which gave rise to most misunderstandings, especially in the English-speaking world, though also in France, because it was thought that this relationship was quite arbitrary. My feeling was, on the contrary, that there was not only one relationship but two different kinds of relationship - one of similarity and an other of contiguity - and that, as a matter of fact, they were actually the same. But that I did not understand right away, and it was the relation of similarity which struck me first. I shall try to explain it in the following way.

In regard to the similarity aspect, my main point was that, exactly as in a musical score, it is impossible to understand a myth as a continuous sequence. This is why we should be aware that if we try to read a myth as we read a novel or a newspaper article, that is line after line, reading from left to right, we don't understand the myth, because we have to apprehend it as a totality and discover that the basic meaning of the myth is not conveyed by the sequence of events but - if I may say so - by bundles of events even although these events appear at different moments in the story. Therefore, we have to read the myth more or less as we would read an orchestral score, not stave after stave, but understanding that we should apprehend the whole page and understand that something which was written on the first stave at the top of the page acquires meaning only if one considers that it is part and parcel of what is written below on the second stave, the third stave, and so on. That is, we have to read not only from left to right, but at the same time vertically, from top to bottom. We have to understand that each page is a totality. And it is only by treating the myth as if it were an orchestral score, written stave after stave, that we can understand it as a totality, that we can extract the meaning out of the myth.

Why and how does this happen? My feeling is that it is the second aspect, the aspect of contiguity, which gives us the significant clue. As a matter of fact, it was about the time when mythical thought - I would not say vanished or disappeared - but passed to the background in western thought during the Renaissance and the seventeenth century, that the first novels began to appear instead of stories still built on the model of mythology. And it was exactly at that time that we witnessed the appearance of the great musical styles characteristic of the seventeenth and, mostly, the eighteenth and nineteenth centuries.

It is exactly as if music had completely changed its traditional shape in order to take over the function - the intellectual as well as emotive function - which mythical thought was giving up more or less at the same period. When I speak here of music, I should, of course, qualify the term. The music that took over the traditional function of mythology is not any kind of music, but music as it appeared in western civilization in the early seventeenth century with Frescobaldi and in the early eighteenth century with Bach, music which reached its full development with Mozart, Beethoven, and Wagner in the eighteenth and nineteenth centuries.

What I would like to do in order to clarify this statement is to offer a concrete example, which I shall take from Wagner's tetralogy, *The Ring*. One of the most important musical themes in the tetralogy is the one which we call in French 'le thème de la renunciation à l'amour' - the renunciation of love. As is well known, this theme appears first of all in the *Rhinegold* at the moment when Alberich is told by the Rhine maidens that he can conquer the gold only if he renounces all kind of human love. This very startling musical motif is a sign to Alberich, given at the very moment when he says that he takes the gold but he renounces love once and for all. All this is very clear and simple; it is the literal sense of the theme: Alberich *is* renouncing love.

Now the second striking and important moment when the theme reappears is in the *Valkyrie* in a circumstance which makes it extremely difficult to understand why. At the moment when Siegmund has just discovered that Sieglinde is his sister and has fallen in love with her, and just when they are going to initiate an incestuous relationship, thanks to the sword which is buried in the tree and which Siegmund is going to tear away from the tree – at that moment, the theme of the renunciation of love reappears. This is some kind of a mystery, because at that moment Siegmund is not at all renouncing love – he's doing quite the opposite and knowing love for the first time of his life with his sister Sieglinde.

The third appearance of the theme is also in the *Valkyrie*, in the last act when Wotan, the king of the gods, is condemning his daughter Brunhilde to a very long magical sleep and surrounding her with fire. We could think that Wotan is also renouncing love because he is renouncing his love for his daughter; but this is not very convincing.

Thus you see that we have exactly the same problem as in mythology; that is, we have a theme – here a musical theme instead of a mythological theme – which appears at three different moments in a very long story: once at the beginning, once in the middle, and once at the end, if for the sake of the argument we limit ourselves to the first two operas of *The Ring*. What I would like to show is that the only way of understanding this mysterious reappearance of the theme is, although they seem very different, to put the three events together, to pile them up one over the other, and to try to discover if they cannot be treated as one and the same event.

We can then notice that, on the three different occasions, there is a treasure which has to be pulled away or torn away from what it is bound to. There is the gold, which is stuck in the depths of the Rhine; there is the sword, which is stuck in a tree, which is a symbolic tree, the tree of life or the tree of the universe; and there is the woman Brunhilde, who will have to be pulled out of the fire. The recurrence of the theme then suggests to us that, as a matter of fact, the gold, the sword, and Brunhilde are one and the same: the gold as a means to conquer power, the sword as a means to conquer love, if I may say so. And the fact that we have a kind of coalescence between the gold, the sword, and the woman is, as a matter of fact, the best explanation we have of the reason why, at the end of the *Twilight of the Gods*, it is through Brunhilde that the gold will return to the Rhine; they have been one and the same, but looked at through different angles.

Other points of the plot are also made very clear. For instance, even though Alberich renounced love, he will later on, thanks to the gold, become able to seduce a woman which will bear him a son, Hagen. It is thanks to his conquest of the sword that Siegmund also will beget a son, who will be Siegfried.

Thus the recurrence of the theme shows us something never explained in the poems, that there is a kind of twin relationship between Hagen the traitor and Siegfried the hero. They are in a very close parallelism. This explains also why it will be possible that Siegfried and Hagen, or rather Siegfried first as himself and then under the disguise of Hagen, will at different moments of the story conquer Brunhilde.

I could go on like this for a very long time, but perhaps these examples are sufficient to explain the similarity of method between the analysis of myth and the understanding of music. When we listen to music, we are listening, after all, to something which goes on from a beginning to an end and which develops through time. Listen to a symphony: a symphony has a beginning, has a middle, it has an end, but nevertheless I would not understand anything of the symphony and I would not get any musical pleasure out of it if I were not able, at each moment, to muster what I have listened to before and what I am listening to now, and to remain conscious of the totality of the music. If you take the musical formula of theme and variations, for instance, you can only perceive it and feel it only if for each variation you keep in mind the theme which you listened to first; each variation has a flavour of its own, if unconsciously you can superimpose it on the earlier variation that you have listened to.

Thus there is a kind of continuous reconstruction taking place in the mind of the listener to music or the listener to a mythical story. It's not only a global similarity. It is exactly as if, when inventing the specific musical forms, music had only rediscovered structures which already existed on the mythical level.

For instance, it is very striking that the fugue, as it was formalized in Bach's time, is the true-to-life representation of the working of some specific myths, of the kind where we have two characters or two groups of characters. Let's say one good, the other one bad, for instance, though that is an over-simplification. The story unrolled by the myth is that of one group trying to flee and to escape from the other group of characters; so you have a chase of one group by the other, sometimes group A rejoining group B, sometimes group B escaping – all as in a fugue. You have what we call in French 'le sujet et la réponse.' The antithesis or antiphony continues through the story until both groups are almost confused and confounded – an equivalent to the *stretta* of the fugue; then a final solution or climax of this conflict is offered by a conjugation of the two principles which had been opposed all along during the myth. It could be a conflict between the powers above and the powers below, the sky and the earth, or the sun and subterranean powers, on the like. The mythic solution of conjugation is very similar in structure to the chords which resolve and end the musical piece, for they offer also a conjugation of extremes which, for once and at last, are being reunited. It could be shown also that there are myths, or groups of myths, which are constructed like a sonata, or a symphony, or a rondo, or a toccata, or any of all the musical forms which music did not really invent but borrowed unconsciously from the structure of the myth.

There is a little story I would like to tell you. When I was writing *The Raw and the Cooked*, I decided to give each section of the volume the character of a musical form and to call one 'sonata,' another 'rondo,' and so on. I then came upon a myth, the structure of which I could very well understand, but I was unable to find a musical form which would correspond to this mythical structure. So I called my friend the composer, René Leibowitz, and explained to him my problem. I told him the strucutre of the myth: at the beginning two entirely different stories, apparently without any relationship with each other, progressively become intertwined and merge, until at the end they make up only one theme. What would you call a musical piece with the same structure? He thought it over and told me that in the whole history of music there was no musical piece he knew of with that structure. So there is no name for it. It was obviously quite possible to have a musical piece with this structure; and a few weeks later he sent me a score which he had composed and which borrowed the structure of the myth I had explained to him.

Now, the comparison between music and language is an extremely tricky one, because to some extent the comparison is extremely close and there are, at the same time, tremendous differences. For example, contemporary linguists have told us that the basic elements of language are phonemes – that is, those sounds that we represent, incorrectly, by the use of letters – which have no meaning in themselves, but which are combined in order to differentiate meaning. You could say practically the same thing of the musical notes. A note – A, B, C, D, and so on – has no meaning in itself; it is just a note. It is only the combination of the notes which can create music. So you could very well say that, while in language we have phonemes as elementary material, in music we would have something which in French I would call 'soneme' – in English perhaps 'toneme' would do. This is a similarity.

But if you think of the next step or the next level in language, you will find that phonemes are combined in order to make words; and words in their turn are combined together to make sentences. But in music there are no words: the elementary materials – the notes – are combined together, but what you have right away is a 'sentence,' a melodic phrase. So, while in language you have three very definite levels – phonemes combined to make words, words combined to make sentences – in music you have with the notes something of the same kind as phonemes from a logical point of view, but you miss the word level and you go directly to a sentence.

Now you can compare mythology both to music and to language, but there is this difference: in mythology there are no phonemes; the lowest elements are words. So if we take language as a paradigm, the paradigm is constituted by, first, phonemes; second, words; third, sentences. In music you have the equivalent to phonemes and the equivalent to sentences, but you don't have the equivalent to words. In myth you have an equivalent to words, an equivalent to sentences, but you have no equivalent to phonemes. So there is, in both cases, one level missing.

If we try to understand the relationship between language, myth, and music, we can only do so by using language as the point of departure, and then it can be shown that music on the one hand and mythology on the other both stem from languages but grow apart in different directions, that music emphasizes the sound aspect already embedded in language, while mythology emphasizes the sense aspect, the meaning aspect, which is also embedded in language.

It was Ferdinand de Saussure who showed us that language is made up of indissociable elements which are on the one hand the sound and on the other the meaning. And my friend Roman Jakobson has just published a little book which is entitled *Le Son et le Sens*, as the two inseparable faces of language. You have sound, the sound has a meaning, and no meaning can exist without a sound to express it. In music, it is the sound element which takes over, and in the myth it is the meaning element.

I have always dreamed since childhood about being a composer or, at least, an orchestra leader. I tried very hard when I was a child to compose the music for an opera for which I had written the libretto and painted the sets, but I was utterly unable to do so because there is something lacking in my brain. I feel that only music and mathematics can be said to be really innate, and that one must have some genetic apparatus to do either. I remember quite well how, when

I was living in New York during the war as a refugee, I had dinner once with the great French composer, Darius Milhaud. I asked him, 'When did you realize that you were going to be a composer?' He explained to me that, when he was a child in bed slowly falling to sleep, he was listening and hearing a kind of music with no relationship whatsoever to the kind of music he knew; he discovered later that this was already his own music.

Since I was struck by the fact that music and mythology were, if I may say so, two sisters, begotten by language, who had drawn apart, each going in a different direction - as in mythology, one character goes north, the other south, and they never meet again - then, if I wasn't able to compose with sounds, perhaps I would be able to do it with meanings.

The kind of parallelism I have tried to draw - I have said it already but I would like to emphasize it once again - applies only, as far as I am aware, to western music as it developed during the recent centuries. But now we are witnessing something which, from a logical point of view, is very similar to what took place when myth disappeared as a literary genre and was replaced by the novel. We are witnessing the disappearance of the novel itself. And it is quite possible that what took place in the eighteenth century when music took over the structure and function of mythology is now taking place again, in that the so-called serial music has taken over the novel as a genre at the moment when it is disappearing from the literary scene.